HEAVEN

Heaven

An Illustrated History of
the Higher Realms

TIMOTHY FREKE

GODSFIELD PRESS

Dedicated to
Grandma Perham, George, Simon,
and all my other friends
in heaven.

Copyright © 1996 Godsfield Press

Text © 1996 Timothy Freke
Illustration © 1996 Lorraine Harrison

Originally published by Godsfield Press 1996

DESIGNED AND PRODUCED BY
THE BRIDGEWATER BOOK COMPANY LTD

Picture research by Vanessa Fletcher

ISBN 1-899434-36-4

The author and publishers are grateful to the following
for the use of illustrations: Bridgeman Art Library,
Jane Couldrey, Derby Museum and Art Gallery,
e.t. archive, Giraudon/Bridgeman.

Write to:
GODSFIELD PRESS
Laurel House, Station Approach, New Alresford, Hants SO24 9JH

The right of Timothy Freke to be identified as the author
of this work has been asserted by him in accordance
with the Copyright, Design and Patents Act 1988.

A CIP catalogue record for this book is
available from the British Library.

Printed and bound in Singapore by Tien Wah Press

CONTENTS

INTRODUCTION

ANGEL PLAYING THE LUTE
Rosso Fiorentino 1494–1540

NOTHING IS MORE certain in life than death. Yet nothing is more uncertain than what fate, if any, may lie in wait for us after death. Is there a heaven, and if so what will it be like? Will everyone be admitted, or only the chosen few? Where is this paradise and how do we get there? Will it last for all eternity, or is it a stopping-off place between a succession of human lives? Will we get to see our loved ones again, or is heaven only a wish-fulfilling fantasy? Throughout history, people of every culture have asked such questions, and this book explores some of the many diverse answers.

There is an almost universal belief in some sort of afterlife, even in the modern West. Gallup opinion polls have consistently found that around 70 percent of North Americans believe in heaven. The ancients pictured paradise as an idealized version of their earthly existence; a bountiful harvest; luxury and sensual delights; freedom from want and responsibility. Things have not changed that much. Respondents to a questionnaire in a modern periodical called *The U.S. Catholic* saw heaven as "lots of baseball and beautiful scenery," "meeting loved ones again," "getting what you want," and "being able to hug God."

For some, however, the conventional Christian vision of heaven sounds more like hell! The British Prime Minister Lloyd George related:

When I was a boy, the thought of Heaven used to frighten me more than the thought of Hell. I pictured heaven as a place where there would be perpetual Sundays with perpetual services, from which there would be no escape, as the Almighty, assisted by cohorts of angels, would always be on the look-out for those who did not attend. It was a horrible nightmare. The conventional Heaven, with its angels perpetually singing etc., nearly drove me mad in my youth and made me an atheist for ten years.

WHAT HAPPENS AFTER DEATH IS SO UNSPEAKABLY GLORIOUS THAT OUR IMAGINATION AND FEELINGS DO NOT SUFFICE TO FORM EVEN AN APPROXIMATE CONCEPTION OF IT.

Carl Jung
Memories, Dreams and Reflections

But, as this book demonstrates, this austere picture is only one among a myriad of colorful heavenly visions. Perhaps, as the American poet Walt Whitman says:

To die is different from what one supposes — and luckier

ANGEL STANDING IN A STORM
J. M. W. Turner 1775–1851

WHAT IS HEAVEN LIKE?

WHERE IS HEAVEN?

ANY PEOPLE THINK of heaven as somewhere "up in the sky." We refer to the starry night as "the heavens," and the picture of an angel sitting on a cloud playing a harp is a familiar image. In the Old Testament, God is sometimes called "Heaven"; the sky is his throne, the stars are his mantle, and the earth his footstool.

It is natural to locate a spiritual realm in the "heavens above"; from the sky comes life-sustaining warmth and rain, and dramatic lightning, thunder, and wind; the stars are mysterious and infinite, like God, and their movements are predictably consistent, giving a sense of permanence in an ever-changing world.

It has often been presumed, however, that heaven is a place somewhere here on earth. The Garden of Eden was believed by some Christians to be north of Babylon in the Armenian Mountains, where Noah's ark came to rest after the flood. "Bralgu," the Aboriginal land of the dead, is said to be

ANGELS IN A HEAVENLY LANDSCAPE,
FROM THE JOURNEY OF THE MAGI CYCLE
Benozzo di Lese di Sandro Gozzoli 1420–97

in the Gulf of Carpentaria. The Hopi of America believe that Kotluwalawa, the village of the dead, lies at the bottom of Lake Whispering Waters.

The Ngaaju of Borneo hold that the dead go to "Lewu Liau," a village of spirits situated in a lovely fertile country near a river full of fish and a wood filled with game. The Daribi of New Guinea believe that heaven is in an unvisitable lake at the source of a great river. The Trobriand Islanders of New Guinea say that the village of death is only a little way off from their own neighborhood.

THE BUDDHIST HEAVENLY REALM
Jane Couldrey

The Dusun of Borneo situate the abode of the dead on a high mountain. Tantric Hindus believe that heaven is on Mount Kailasa in Tibet, where the god Shiva and his beautiful consort Parvati enjoy sex for all eternity. Other Hindus say that there are many heavens hidden in the clouds surrounding the legendary Mount Meru, somewhere to the north of the Himalayas. They believe that this colossal peak is the center of the Universe, around which the stars revolve.

THE SITUATION OF PARADISE IS SHUT OFF FROM THE WORLD BY MOUNTAINS, OR SEAS, OR SOME TORRID REGION, WHICH CANNOT BE CROSSED; AND SO PEOPLE WHO HAVE WRITTEN ABOUT TOPOGRAPHY MAKE NO MENTION OF IT.

St. Thomas Aquinas
Summa Theologica

In the *Book of Enoch*, an apocryphal Jewish work of the later centuries B.C., God's throne is a high mountain. In *The Pilgrim's Progress*, John Bunyan pictures a heavenly city on a towering hill beyond Jordan, the river of death. In his *Paradisio*, Dante (1265–1321) describes paradise on the summit of the Mountain of Purgatory, that he situates in the middle of an imagined ocean covering the whole of the Southern Hemisphere.

The Tasmanians of Australia believe that the dead travel to a nearby island. The Celts held that the heavenly "Tir na n'Oc" was an island, that they believed to be on the other side of a great ocean. Plutarch, the priest of Apollo at Delphi (second century A.D.), thought that the Island of the Blessed was five days' sail from Britain.

Depressed by first-century B.C. Roman decadence, Horace suggested setting sail for heaven. Sixteen centuries later, Columbus actually did so. He believed the earth was pear-shaped and that heaven was at the tip, "like a nipple on a woman's breast." When he discovered America he hoped to find paradise. In 1595, Sir Walter Raleigh's expedition experienced the mighty currents of the Orinoco, which were so powerful that they believed they must have found one of the four rivers of Eden.

SILENTLY, ONE BY ONE,
IN THE INFINITE MEADOWS OF HEAVEN,
BLOSSOMED THE LOVELY STARS.
THE FORGET-ME-NOTS OF THE ANGELS.

Henry Wadsworth Longfellow

LUGH, SUN GOD OF THE IRISH CELTS
Michael Macliamoir

WHAT IS HEAVEN?

OST VISIONS of heaven reflect the aspirations and achievements of the cultures from which they come. Only for nomadic peoples, like the natives of North America, is heaven seen as wild, like nature. For settled societies, heaven bears the mark of human civilization. Even paradises like Eden are not natural habitats, but resemble cultivated gardens within which God walks at his pleasure, like a wealthy landowner.

Heaven has often been pictured as a fabulous city. The Aztecs of South America believed in the "Mansions of the Sun" inhabited by dead priests and nobles. Some Ancient Greeks imagined a glorious city of jewels paved with ivory and encircled by a river of perfume. Plato claimed that the pattern of the ideal city is laid up in heaven "which he who desires may behold, and beholding, may set his own in order."

St. Paul says: "we have no lasting city, but we seek the city that is to come." St. Augustine writes of the "City of God." In *The Pilgrim's Progress*, Bunyan describes it as built of pearls and jewels, and glittering in the sun. The Book of Revelation says that the radiance of the heavenly Jerusalem is of "a most rare jewel, like jasper and clear as crystal." Its streets are paved with gold, so fine that it is as transparent as glass. Its walls are of precious stones, and its twelve city gates are each a single pearl.

PARADISE OF THE SYMBOLIC FOUNDATION
Dirck Bouts c.1415—75

Otto of Freising (d.1158) searches for a mystical interpretation of this vision:

We can imagine how magnificent our lives would be in this heavenly fatherland! For if it is beautiful and magnificent when taken in the literal sense, how much more beautiful and magnificent does it appear understood in a spiritual sense.

This view of heaven "understood in a spiritual sense" became known as the "Beatific Vision"; the sublime experience of being in the presence of God, when, as Pope Benedict XII put it in 1336:

THE PALACE OF THE EVERLASTING KING, WHERE IS LIFE WITHOUT DEATH, DAY WITHOUT NIGHT, TRUTH WITHOUT FALSEHOOD, JOY WITHOUT SORROW, SURENESS WITHOUT DREAD, REST WITHOUT TRAVAIL, EVERLASTINGNESS WITHOUT END.

St. Mary of Oignies

Souls behold the divine essence with intuitive and face-to-face vision...the divine essence immediately showing itself to them without covering, clearly and openly.

The early Christian Gnostics also saw the heavenly goal as mystical knowledge of divine Truth. In Jewish thought, this was sometimes envisioned literally as a heavenly academy in which scholars and rabbis studied the Scriptures. In Christian art this vision has been famously portrayed in the Vatican Palace, where Raphael (1483–1520) painted a heaven populated by a school of blessed doctors.

Jesus, however, said, "The kingdom of heaven is within you," suggesting that he did not conceive of it as a place, but rather as an inner state of awareness. In the same spirit, the Islamic Sufi poet Omar Khayyám

PARADISE GARDEN
Meister Oberrheinischer

concluded, "I myself am heaven and hell," and Voltaire declared, "Paradise is where I am."

In the Gnostic Gospel of Thomas, Jesus is asked by a disciple, "When will the Kingdom of Heaven come?" He replies, "Not by waiting for it. The Kingdom of Heaven is laid out upon the earth and men do not see it." From this perspective, held by the great mystics of the world, heaven is not a place that awaits us after death; it is a spiritual awareness available to us right now, which transforms earth into paradise and allows us to see, as the poet Elizabeth Barrett Browning says, that:

Earth's crammed with heaven,
And every common bush afire with God.

WHAT IS HEAVEN LIKE?

A REST BETWEEN LIVES

*F*OR HINDUS AND BUDDHISTS, heaven is not for all eternity, but only a resting place between lives, where souls prepare for their next human incarnation. If they have lived a good life, the dead enjoy the pleasures of heaven for "a period proportionate to the merit of their being." Eventually a soul's "karma," the fears and desires left unresolved from its previous life, draws it back into another earthly existence. The ultimate bliss of "liberation" lies beyond the wheel of death and rebirth. It is even beyond heaven.

Belief in reincarnation is not found just in the great Eastern religions. Many Native American, African, and other Aboriginal peoples expect to return to this world after a stay in heaven, as did most of the ancients. Plutarch, a priest of the Greek god Apollo, speaks of souls "ordained to wander between incarnations," and of advanced souls called "genii," who dwell in the higher realms of heaven and assist in initiatory rites. The Greek philosopher Pythagoras claimed to be able to remember all of his past lives.

The Ancient Egyptian sage Hermes Trismegistus says:

Not all human souls, but only the pious, are divine. Once separated from the body, and after the struggle to acquire piety, which consists in knowing God and injuring none, such a soul becomes all intelligence. The impious soul, however, punishes itself by seeking another human body to enter into.

The Roman historian Josephus reports that the Jewish Pharisees also believed in reincarnation but believed that only the souls of good men were reincarnated, while the bad endured eternal punishment.

Belief in reincarnation was widespread among early Christian Gnostics, until these beliefs were ruthlessly suppressed by the dogmatic Roman Church. And many esoteric schools of Islam, like the Ismailis, believe in "Rij'at," the rebirth of the Iman, their spiritual leader, after death, and in

THUS THE SEER,
  WITH VISION CLEAR,
SEES FORM APPEAR AND DISAPPEAR,
  IN PERPETUAL ROUND AND STRANGE,
MYSTERIOUS CHANGE,
  FROM BIRTH TO DEATH, FROM DEATH TO BIRTH;
FROM EARTH TO HEAVEN, FROM HEAVEN TO EARTH;
  TILL GLIMPSES MORE SUBLIME,
OF THINGS, UNSEEN BEFORE,
  UNTO HIS WONDERING EYES REVEAL,
THE UNIVERSE, AS AN IMMEASURABLE WHEEL,
  TURNING FOREVERMORE,
IN THE RAPID AND RUSHING RIVER OF TIME.

Henry Wadsworth Longfellow
"Rain in Summer'

WHAT IS HEAVEN LIKE?

HEAVENLY WINDS

HEAVEN

"Tanasukh," the reincarnation of the souls of ordinary men. According to Hebrew Kabbalists, the night-angel Layela invokes amnesia of past lives by giving the soul a little pinch on the nose while applying light pressure to the upper lip, where we all bear the marks of the angel's finger tips.

In some traditions, the soul's holiday in heaven is only brief. The Greek philosopher Plato, however, says that, save for certain exceptions, the soul remains in heaven awaiting rebirth for "many revolutions of ages." The *Bhagavad Gita*, a Hindu scripture, also speaks of an "immensity of years between lives." The Roman poet Virgil (70–19 B.C.) mentions a thousand-year cycle of rebirth. The Greek historian Herodotus (484–424 B.C.) talks of three thousand years in the afterdeath state. Heaven is seen as a place of assimilation. Life is like eating a meal, which may be done quickly; death is like digestion, which takes much longer.

AENAES PERCEIVED BEFORE HIM A SPACIOUS VALLEY, WITH TREES GENTLY WAVING IN THE WIND, A TRANQUIL LANDSCAPE, THROUGH WHICH THE RIVER LETHE FLOWED. ALONG THE BANKS OF THE STREAM WANDERED A COUNTLESS MULTITUDE, NUMEROUS AS INSECTS IN THE AIR. AENEAS, WITH SURPRISE, ENQUIRED WHO WERE THESE. ANCHISES ANSWERED, "THEY ARE SOULS TO WHICH BODIES ARE TO BE GIVEN IN DUE TIME. MEANWHILE THEY DWELL ON LETHE'S BANK AND DRINK OF THE OBLIVION OF THEIR FORMER LIVES."

Virgil
Aeneid

For traditions that believe in reincarnation, we have all visited heaven many times already and will probably return to earth in many more lives to come. The Dalai Lama, leader of the Tibetan Buddhists, says, "Treat everyone as if they were already your friend, because in a past life they probably have been!"

THE INHABITANTS OF HEAVEN

CELESTIAL HOSTS

*I*N THE MONOTHEISTIC religions of Judaism, Christianity, and Islam, angels play a similar role to the many gods and goddesses of polytheistic traditions. They are God's holy court in heaven and oversee his Creation. We have come to imagine them as androgynous winged figures, but originally most of them were more like humans. Jacob, in his famous dream, saw them ascending to and descending from heaven on a giant ladder, not flying with celestial wings. In Genesis it even says they made love with the beautiful "daughters of men."

"Angel" means "messenger." Many pagans thought that birds were messengers of the gods, and as more and more pagans converted to Christianity, angels were increasingly imagined as having bird-like wings to accommodate this older belief. The Ancient Greek word "psyche" means both "soul" and "butterfly"; after death the soul was seen as emerging from

the physical body, like a butterfly freed from its chrysalis. We have inherited this image in our picture of the dead as winged angels.

To the Jews, the heavenly angels were mighty and awe-inspiring powers; even the Cherubim, which have come down to us today as chubby little boys with wings, playing trumpets on Christmas cards, inspired awe. In fact "Cherubim" means "fullness of God's knowledge," and they were among the most powerful of the celestial hosts. Satan himself was originally a Cherubim. The medieval Christian mystic Jan van Ruysbrock claimed that the Cherubim are so heavenly that they "dwell with us only when, above all conflict, we are with God in peace, in contemplation, and in perennial love."

The poet Rainer Maria Rilke said, "Every angel is terrifying." Certainly this is true of Islamic angels. Israfil, "The Burning One," is the Angel of Day. He sings praises to Allah with myriad tongues in a thousand different languages. From his breath, Allah creates a million more angels to glorify Himself. Each day and night, Israfil looks down towards hell and weeps such tears that "would inundate the earth if Allah did not stop the flow." He is also the angel of music and his horn contains dwellings like a honeycomb, within which rest the souls of the dead.

> BUT IF ONE ARCHANGEL
> NOW, PERILOUSLY, FROM
> BEHIND THE STARS
> TOOK EVEN ONE STEP
> DOWN TOWARD US: OUR
> OWN HEART, BEATING
> HIGHER AND HIGHER,
> WOULD BEAT TO DEATH.
> WHO ARE YOU?
>
> *Rainer Maria Rilke*
> *Duino Elegies 2*

Azrael, the Angel of Death, is said to be hidden by a million veils. He has four faces, 70,000 wings, and his body is covered in eyes. Whenever one of these eyes blinks, a creature dies. Djibril, known to Christians as Gabriel, is the angel who brought the Koran to Mohammed. His hair is saffron, and the sun sits between his eyes. He dives into the ocean 365 times a day, and when he re-emerges the millions of drops of water that fall from his 1,600 wings are transformed by Allah into yet more angels.

The fifth-century Christian theologian known as Pseudo-Dionysius claimed that there were originally 399,920,004 angels; but one-third of these joined Satan, leaving exactly 266,613,336 angels in heaven. He divided these into nine choirs, which became the "nine bright shiners" of old folk songs. Christians in the Middle Ages became obsessed with obscure details about angels. They even had serious theological disputes about how many could fit on a pinhead. Very few, according to one theologian, who claimed that angels could tower 96 miles high.

The Swedish mystic and scientist Emanuel Swedenborg (1688–1772), claimed to have been taken to heaven, and to have talked often with angels. He said spirits and angels were invisible to us because they were not composed of material substances and therefore could not reflect the light of the sun. But "when it is the Lord's good pleasure, the good spirits appear to others, and each other, like bright lucid stars."

Angels are not seen only as the spiritual powers of paradise. They are also believed to surround us invisibly here on earth, to guide us towards our heavenly home. As the saying goes:

Be not afraid to have strangers in your house,
for some thereby have entertained angels.

THE RAMPARTS OF GOD'S HOUSE
John Melhuish Strudwick 1849–1937

BIZARRE BEASTS AND GIANT PLANTS

*W*HETHER WITH TERRIFYING ANGELS, the mutant beasts of the Christian Book of Revelation, or the ancient pagan gods or goddesses that preside over the dead, heaven is often portrayed as populated by some very bizarre beings. In Tibetan tradition, for example, the judgement of the soul is supervised by Shinje, a monkey-headed god. In ancient Eygptian tradition this role is fulfilled by Thoth, also sometimes pictured with a monkey's head, but more often with that of an ibis, a type of wading bird. Many heavens are home to both strange animals and plants. In Tir Taingin, the Celtic Land of Promise, we are told of otherworldly cows with red ears, and of horses of sky blue, or with four green legs.

THE SUPREME PERSONALITY OF GODHEAD

AND BEFORE THE THRONE THERE WAS A SEA OF GLASS LIKE UNTO CRYSTAL; AND IN THE MIDST OF THE THRONE, AND ROUND ABOUT THE THRONE, WERE FOUR BEASTS FULL OF EYES BEFORE AND BEHIND.

AND THE FIRST BEAST WAS LIKE A LION, AND THE SECOND BEAST WAS LIKE A CALF, AND THE THIRD BEAST HAD A FACE AS A MAN, AND THE FOURTH BEAST WAS LIKE A FLYING EAGLE.

AND THE FOUR BEASTS HAD EACH OF THEM SIX WINGS ABOUT THEM; AND THEY WERE FULL OF EYES WITHIN.

The Revelation of
St. John the Divine

Some Muslims believe there is a tree in paradise so big that a man could ride beneath its shade for a year and not come to the end of it. Likewise, a colossal rose tree is said to grow around the Hindu Mount Meru and give shade to the whole earth; its fruit are as big as elephants and their juice forms the river of immortality.

The Buddhist heaven known as "The Pure Land" is described as covered with lotus flowers:

Some of the lotus flowers are half a mile in circumference, others up to ten miles. And from each jewel lotus issue 36,000 rays. And at the the end of each ray there issue 36,000 buddhas, with golden bodies, who bear the thirty-two marks of the superman.

INHABITANTS OF HEAVEN
Jane Couldrey

HEAVENLY HIERARCHIES

ANY ANCIENT cultures believed that heaven was reserved for important people, like nobles and priests. Christian theologians and artists have often portrayed a celestial hierarchy of famous saints and martyrs surrounding God, like a court around an earthly king. The ancient Chinese saw heaven as a divine government, similar to a state bureaucracy.

Those who died after an exemplary life could reach high office in the otherworldly administration, while others would become laborers or prisoners. Eternity was spent gaining status and rising through the ranks. In one Chinese tomb archaeologists found an official letter to a heavenly administrator, with a request to forward it to the Lord of Death, as a reference for the dead man. Mount T'ai was said to be the seat of this heavenly bureaucracy. Here were kept jade tablets, which recorded in duplicate detailed information concerning both the living and the dead. The god of Mount T'ai, the "grandson of the Heavenly Emperor," ruled the "forecourt of heaven and the earthly branch of the bureaucracy of destiny." Ssu-ming, the "Director of Destinies," held the power to lengthen or shorten life, and some saints were said to have journeyed to Mount T'ai to petition him for a longer life.

AT CLASSICAL CONCERTS IN ENGLAND YOU WILL FIND ROWS OF WEARY PEOPLE WHO ARE THERE NOT BECAUSE THEY REALLY LIKE CLASSICAL MUSIC, BUT BECAUSE THEY THINK THEY OUGHT TO LIKE IT. WELL, THERE IS THE SAME THING IN HEAVEN. A NUMBER OF PEOPLE SIT THERE IN GLORY, NOT BECAUSE THEY ARE HAPPY, BUT BECAUSE THEY THINK THEY OWE IT TO THEIR POSITION TO BE IN HEAVEN. THEY ARE ALMOST ALL ENGLISH.

George Bernard Shaw
Man and Superman

THE LAST JUDGEMENT
Hieronymus Bosch c.1450–1516

REUNITED IN HEAVEN

*I*T IS A COMMON hope that in heaven we will once again meet our departed loved ones. Many people who have had a near-death experience, in which they have clinically died and yet returned to life with wonderful tales of the hereafter, claim to have talked in heaven with deceased friends and family. But, if we do get to be with our parents again, and if they also get to be with theirs, and so on, then the columnist Bob Ripley has calculated that in twenty generations there will be 1,048,576 souls, all hoping to be together – not counting friends, husbands, wives, and other family! These colossal numbers will be lessened, of course, if only the worthy are allowed into heaven, while others endure purgatory, or even hell. But how will we be able to enjoy eternal happiness in heaven if our loved ones happen to be in the "other place?" A twelfth-century monk from Elsham near Oxford, who claims to have visited heaven in a vision, replies that we will "not miss the damned, because there will be no attachment to anyone unworthy." William King, Bishop of Dublin in 1702, suggests that it might be a pleasure to see them suffer from the safe distance of heaven, because it will remind us of our own escape. Do husbands and wives get reunited in heaven, and if so, what happens to those who have married many times?

> THERE, ALSO, WE SHALL MEET WITH THOUSANDS AND THOUSANDS THAT HAVE GONE BEFORE US TO THAT PLACE; NONE OF THEM HURTFUL, BUT LOVING HOLY, EVERYONE WALKING IN THE SIGHT OF GOD, AND STANDING IN HIS PRESENCE WITH ACCEPTANCE FOR EVER.
>
> *John Bunyan*
> The Pilgrim's
> Progress

Jesus answered this dilemma by saying that in heaven there is no marriage. According to some Christian traditions, there is no death in heaven, so there is no need of birth or carnal love; the dead are asexual, like the angels. Some have said that women, if they get allowed into heaven at all, get transmuted into men. St. Augustine thought they remained women, but this was not dangerous because "all lust will then be extinguished." Some Islamic traditions have simply denied that women possess souls at all, and so could not possibly go to heaven.

Certain Hindu sects believe that, although we seem to meet our loved ones, we are actually alone in heaven. The Theosophist William Judge says:

> ...it is sometimes asked, what of those we have left behind? Do we see them there? We do not see them there in fact, but we make ourselves their images as full, complete and objective as in life, and devoid of all that we then thought was a blemish. We live with them and see them grow great and good instead of mean or bad... This is for the benefit of the soul. You may call it a delusion if you will, but the illusion is necessary to happiness, just as it often is in life.

This does not explain, however, remarkable testimonies like that of an American woman who claims to have visited heaven during a near-death experience. There she met departed family, including a baby brother of whose existence she was unaware. She was told that the brother was appearing as a baby for her benefit, but that in heaven everyone is actually always in their prime. Upon regaining consciousness, she questioned her elderly mother and was astonished to discover that she had indeed had a brother who died as a baby, and who had never been talked of.

ANGELS PLAYING MUSICAL INSTRUMENTS
Francesco Botticini c.1446–97

GETTING INTO HEAVEN

OR ANCIENT hierarchical cultures, like the early Egyptians and the Aztecs, only those with social standing were allowed into paradise. In warrior cultures, like those of the Nordic peoples, women and children were excluded from heaven, which was reserved for brave men. The Evae of the Pacific Islands held that only warriors who died in battle, and the women folk who supported them, could ascend to the heavenly "Red Place" in the sky, while the rest were doomed to permanent estrangement in an earthbound "Place of Brown."

The leader of the infamous Islamic Assassins created a heaven on earth of hashish and sex for the young men that were his disciples, promising them a similar eternal heaven if they performed acts of terror on his behalf. In the Crusades of the Middle Ages, both the Christian and Muslim combatants were promised heaven for butchering each other. Even in the Second World War, the Shinto religion of Japan promised suicidal kamikaze pilots that they would become gods.

For the Raiteans of Tahiti, getting to heaven is just a matter of luck; whether the dead go to "Ao," the Light, or "Po," the Darkness, simply

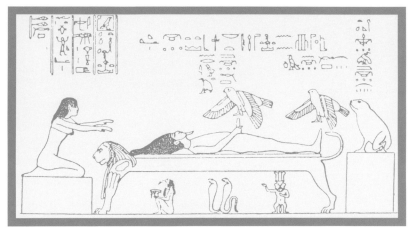

OSIRIS, THE ANCIENT EGYPTIAN GOD OF DEATH

depends on the soul happening to perch itself on the right rock. And a deceased Muju of the Melanesian Islands is believed to travel precariously on the back of a great serpent called Mortetutau to the paradise of Tum, where he will enjoy an endless supply of foods and intoxicants; but only if an "inexorable old woman" finds the requisite two lines of tattooing on one of his arms.

In most traditions, however, entrance to heaven is a reward for a good life. The Greek poet Pindar, in 5 B.C., believed that three successive lives of great purity were needed.

To decide who gets into heaven, some sort of judgement is often imagined. For the Ancient Egyptians, the heart of the deceased was weighed against the Feather of Truth, in the Hall of Maat; only if they balanced would the soul join the sun-god Ra on his journey across the skies. Similarly, in the *Tibetan Book of the Dead*, the god Yama weighs black and white pebbles, representing the soul's good and bad actions in life. Sometimes this judgement is symbolized as an arduous journey to heaven, which the unworthy fail to make. Some Egyptians believed that the dead must try and climb a ladder of slanting sunbeams, and some Africans talk of ascending a rope. In the North of England the dead were buried with their boots on to help them cross Whinnymuir, a wild land covered in gorse, brambles, thorns, and flinty stones; eventually they reached Brig O'Dread, a bridge "no broader than a thread," which led to heaven. The living often burnt candles, so that the dead could see their way more easily .

In the Zoroastrian religion, the righteous dead are greeted by a fragrant wind and meet a beautiful maiden, "the embodiment of pure thoughts, pure words and pure deeds." She leads the righteous to Amesh-spentas, the golden seat of Ahura Mazda. The dead must travel across the Bridge of the Separator, which gets narrower and narrower, until the wicked fall to their doom. Similarly, the Muslims have a bridge called al-Sirat, which is "thinner than a hair and sharper than a sword." This bridge spans hell, from which flames roar up, and into which the wicked tumble. Angels help the good to make the crossing, which is a type of purgatory and can take as long as 25,000 years.

Other traditions suggest a more effortless journey. The Egyptians were ferried over the Lily Lake to the other world, as were the Greeks and Romans across the River Styx to Hades. The Greeks also talked of the souls of the pious floating up like specks of dust into the air; purified by wind, water, and fire, they travel to the moon, where they find the heavenly Elysian Fields. Some pure souls go even higher to the sun, or higher still, becoming stars in the Milky Way. For Egyptians, the Milky Way was the road to heaven; the soul soared into the sky as a falcon or goose, or traveled on the back of a grasshopper, or in clouds, or fumes of incense. Many Christian saints have also reportedly been taken up to heaven on a cloud.

THOSE WHO HAVE PERFORMED WORKS OF VIRTUE, WALKING IN PIETY, HAVE KEPT GOOD CONSCIENCE, ARE TAKEN UP BY ANGELS AND BROUGHT FROM THE STREAM OF BURNING FIRE, INTO A LIFE FULL OF BLISS AND JOY, WHERE THE ETERNAL PATH OF THE MIGHTY GOD LEADS AND TRIPLE SPRINGS OF WINE AND MILK AND HONEY FLOW...
THERE ARE NO SERVANTS THERE AND NO MASTERS; THERE ARE NO PRINCES, AND ALL ARE EQUAL BEFORE THE MOST HIGH.

The Christian
Sibyline Oracle

VISITORS TO HEAVEN

OCCASIONALLY HEAVEN is visited by the living. Dante gives us a metaphorical account in his *Paradisio*. Plato tells the story of Er, who dies in battle and goes to heaven, but is told to return to tell the tale. The twelfth-century monk from Elsham claimed to have visited heaven (but not the highest heaven), which was behind a glorious wall of crystal, so high and long that he could not see its end. He heard music, as if all the bells in the world were pealing, and experienced a wonderful light, with a "brightness, though it were inestimable, nevertheless dulled not a man's sight, but rather sharpened it."

I ON THE ILLUMINATED FLOOR
OF PARADISE HAVE STAYED
AND SEEN WHAT NONE
CAN CALL TO MIND AGAIN
OUTSIDE THE DOOR.
    BECAUSE OUR INTELLECT AS
    IT DRAWS NEAR
DEPTH OF DESIRE IS MADE SO
STILL AND DEEP
    MEMORY LOSES ALL THAT
    ONCE WAS CLEAR.

Dante Paradisio

One of the most extraordinary heavenly visitors was Emanuel Swedenborg, whose life and works became a profound influence on Blake, Goethe, Steiner, and Emerson. He was an eminent Swedish engineer and mathematician, who spoke nine languages and wrote 150 books on seventeen different sciences. Like Leonardo da Vinci, he was a man before his time, whose visionary inventions included an undersea boat, a glider, and an ear trumpet for the deaf; he even foresaw elements of twentieth-century physics.

Swedenborg was a respected and orthodox member of society, who often dined with royalty. However, from the age of forty-five until he died,

SCENES FROM DANTE'S DIVINE COMEDY
Carl Vogel von Vogelstein 1788–1868

GETTING INTO HEAVEN

he found himself continually visited by angels, and allowed to visit heaven:

Today's churchman knows nothing of heaven, hell, or his own life after death. To prevent so negative an attitude... it has been possible for me to be right with angels and talk with them person to person. I have also been allowed to see what heaven is like.

Over many years Swedenborg talked with numerous friends who had died, and with a host of angelic beings, who themselves had once been human and had become angels because of the good lives they had led on earth (although most also required a period of training and purification in the world of spirits). The angels, he reported, "express affection with vowels, ideas with consonants, and total communication with words." They cannot speak "the human language of doubt and conflict."

Swedenborg presented a lively vision of heaven, unlike the rather somber picture that was prevalent at the time. For him, there was only a thin veil between this world and the next. Heaven is the fulfilment of material life, where souls delight in the senses. Human family love and communal concerns replace the grand "beatific vision" of the Church. God is loved, not only directly, but also through the love and charity shown to others.

There are "no idlers in heaven," each soul having a different occupation to suit it. The journey to God is never over, and spiritual development continues without end. The deceased stay as men and women, and "husbands and wives may come together if they wish for a longer or shorter time depending on the truth of their love."

The Church at this time preached that an unbaptized child would not be admitted to heaven, but Swedenborg says that "all children who die throughout the world go to heaven." Indeed, he estimated that one third of the population of paradise were children.

THE ANGEL OF DEATH
Evelyn de Morgan 1850–1919

The soul "lives in the body, not as a bird in a cage, but like water in a sponge," and after death everyone is allowed "to be in delight, whether spirits or angels, even the most unclean who delight in adultery, stealing, blasphemy, lying... Everyone whether good or evil is in his own delight" (although the delight of the evil may be a torment to them).

Even atheists, although "at first bewildered and embarrassed," have a place in the hereafter.

NEAR-DEATH EXPERIENCES

*T*HE POWER OF modern medicine has led to more and more people being brought back to life after having been pronounced clinically dead. Many of these patients claim to have visited the afterlife while "dead," a phenomena that has come to be known as a "near-death experience," or NDE. Although no two experiences are the same, they do exhibit remarkable similarities.

I KEPT THINKING "WELL WHEN I WAS TAKING GEOMETRY, THEY ALWAYS TOLD ME THERE WERE ONLY THREE DIMENSIONS, BUT THEY ARE WRONG. THERE ARE MORE." AND OF COURSE, OUR WORLD — THE ONE WE ARE LIVING IN NOW — IS THREE-DIMENSIONAL, BUT THE NEXT ONE DEFINITELY ISN'T. AND THAT'S WHY IT'S SO HARD TO TELL YOU THIS.

Near-Death Experience
Reflections on
Life after Life

In a typical NDE, patients find themselves outside their own body; they can see in detail the doctors frantically trying to resuscitate them, and can hear worried relatives and friends, often in other parts of the hospital. Suddenly they find themselves moving down a dark tunnel, towards a beautiful, loving light, which is often equated with God, Jesus, or an angel, depending on personal expectations:

The light was so beautiful and radiant, but it didn't hurt my eyes. It's not any kind of light you can describe on earth. I didn't actually see a person in this light, and yet it has a special identity, it definitely does... I felt as though I were surrounded by an overwhelming love and compassion.

They are joined by deceased friends or family, who

ANGEL
Abbott Handerson Thayer 1849–1921

can communicate with them telepathically:

> I realized that all these people were there, almost multitudes it seemed...They
> were all the people I had known in my past life, but who had passed on before. I
> recognized my grandmother, and a girl I had known at school. It seems I mainly
> saw their faces and felt their presence. They all seemed pleased. It was a very happy
> occasion and I felt they had come to protect or to guide me.

Friends, family, or some other guide lead the new arrival into some sort of
wonderful heavenly world:

> I found myself in the most enchanting place you could ever visit. The beauty was
> far beyond anything that I had ever seen before in my life. It was so luxuriant that
> there is absolutely no way to express to you the intense enjoyment I felt with the
> place... I discovered myself drifting down to a huge valley. It sloped downward
> from low, gently rolling hills. There were miles upon miles of flat rolling plains.

Those who go deeply into the near-death experience often report
reviewing everything they have said and done in their lives, but with an
understanding of the consequences of all their choices. Some people
interpret this as an opportunity for self-judgement:

> When the light appeared, the first thing he said to me was, "What have you to
> show me that you've done with your life?"... And that's when the flashbacks
> started. The scenes were just like you walked out and saw them, completely
> three-dimensional and in color.

The near-death experience is not a new phenomenon. The historian Bede
(673–735) records a report from a man who also left his body, saw the

> I SAW CHILDREN PLAYING IN AN AMUSEMENT
> PARK. THEY LOOKED FAMILIAR...THE PARK
> WAS LIKE ONE I REMEMBERED AS A CHILD...
> BUT ALL MY OLD PLAYMATES WERE THERE, JUST
> LIKE THEY WERE SIXTY YEARS AGO...NONE OF
> THEM NOTICED ME; THEY CONTINUED TO PLAY
> IN THE AMUSEMENT PARK AS WE HAD DONE
> HALF A CENTURY AGO...I WAS A LITTLE BOY
> AGAIN, RELIVING MY YOUTH...GOD IT WAS
> BEAUTIFUL.
>
> *Near-Death Experience*
> *Reflections on Life after Life*

Love-Light, and visited heaven:

> *A handsome man in a shining robe was my guide...He soon brought me out of*
> *darkness into an atmosphere of clear light, and he led me forward in bright light.*
> *I saw a tremendous wall which seemed to be infinite in length and height in all*
> *directions... All at once — I know not by what means — we were on top of it. Within*
> *lay a very broad and pleasant meadow... Such was the light flooding all this place*
> *that it seemed greater than the brightness of daylight or of the sun's rays at noon.*

As often happens in an NDE, this man was told that this was not his
time to die, and so he must return to tell the tale, and to live a loving life.
But heaven is so wonderfully blissful that few wish to return of their
own volition.

ANCIENT HEAVENS

NORDIC AND CELTIC HEAVENS

S NORRI STURLUSON, the thirteenth-century Icelandic historian, relates that among the Nordic peoples, only aristocrats and warriors killed in battle gained a glorious afterlife in the heavenly Valhalla, Hall of the Slain, where they became the god Odin's war-band. Eventually, heaven itself would be destroyed, and Odin and his followers would die a final death in a hopeless last stand against the powers of chaos.

Until this "Doom of the Gods," dead warriors feasted on pork from a magical boar that was cooked each night in a cauldron and returned to life each morning. They drank only mead, for it was ridiculous that such men could ever drink water.

As Sturluson was a Christian, however, he also believed that the good would enjoy eternal life with the All-Father in the beautiful hall of Gimle, which was brighter than the sun.

LOLLAN WITH FAIRY LOVE

ANCIENT HEAVENS

MYTHICAL HEAVEN
Jane Couldrey

Among the Celts, the dead were said to live with the fairies, over the sea to the west, or at the bottom of the ocean. "Tir na n'Oc," the Shimmering Land, was the Celtic heaven. It was regarded as the Land of Eternal Youth, or Land of the Living, because only its inhabitants were truly alive. In some old stories it is the Land of Promise, ruled by Manannan, god of sea, magic, and rebirth. Here there was no judgement and no fighting; only love-making, music and song, games, boat races, and beautiful birds singing lullabies to the drowsy. Whatever a soul wished for it would receive, yet magically the desires of its inhabitants never conflicted.

THERE CAN BE SEEN A GOLDEN OTHER-WORLDLY HORSE; TWO FIERCE AND FLASHING EYES HE HAD, AN EXQUISITE PURE CRIMSON MANE, WITH FOUR GREEN LEGS AND A LONG TAIL THAT FLOATED IN WAVY CURLS.

Irish Folk Tale

The Celts believed in reincarnation. It was this strong conviction that Julius Caesar thought made them such formidable warriors. Heaven was merely a resting place on a longer journey of spiritual attainment, the goal of which was Gwenved, the White Heaven. Those who achieved spiritual perfection need not reincarnate again, unless they wished to return to help others, like the bodhisattvas of Buddhist tradition.

ANCIENT
EGYPTIAN HEAVENS

*T*HE ANCIENT EGYPTIAN culture thrived for many thousands of years, so it is not surprising that it had many different myths about heaven. In some, the dead walk a road bordered by flowers, that leads to heaven. In others, the deceased becomes a rower on the barge of the sun-god Ra, as it crosses the sky to its land in the East. The dead are also described as being rowed across the Lily Lake by:

I AM THE SERVANT OF RA, ELDEST SON OF THE MORNING, WASHING THE EYES OF GODS AND BATHING IN TEARS. I AM THE OAR OF HIS BOAT, A STRONG SYCAMORE HEWN FOR ROWING. I AM A FRIEND OF FIRE AND WATER. IN THIS BOAT I CROSS THE LAKE OF FLAME, FERRYING ANCIENT SOULS. NEITHER COLD NOR WET, NOR YOUNG NOR OLD, WE REACH THE MOUNTAIN AND ENTER THE MOMENT. AGAINST THE RED SKY A YOUNG BULL STANDS; SPERM FALLS ON THE STONY PLATEAU. THE GRAPES RIPEN AND GRASSES GROW. HE WHO HAS NO BOAT DISAPPEARS IN THE LAKE OF FLAME. HE HAS NO NAME IN THE MEMORY OF TIME.

Water and Fire
Egyptian Book of the Dead

"He-Who-Looks-Backwards," a ferryman who takes them to the Fields of Earu, the Fields of Rejoicing, where heralds announce their arrival and the gods, in robes and white sandals, come to welcome them.

Earu was seen as a superior copy of Egypt, with its own heavenly Nile. The dead are pictured traveling with the sun-god to see pleasant valleys and cool streams, where they pick flowers and hunt birds. They enjoy a continuation of their earthly life, but with more pleasures and luxuries. In this paradise an aristrocrat could look forward to "living in a comfortable house with a pool and shady trees, with his family, concubines, and slaves around him." Other folk would still be working, irrigating and tilling the celestial fields. The Egyptians were very pious, so the dead were also imagined performing good deeds, including helping the poor during the judgement of the soul.

Other myths talk of Amentet, a country of the dead on the western frontier of Egypt's fertile land, at the edge of the desert where the necropolises were located. The dead were said to live beneath the earth, in a system of caves and passages, where the sun visited them by night. In certain texts, souls go to join The Indestructible Ones, the circumpolar stars, that never set and so were thought never to die.

For the Ancient Egyptians, a person is made up of a "khat," or physical body, that decays after death; a "ka," or soul, which survives death and may reincarnate into another body; and a "ba," which is the spiritual essence, the spark of the sublime unchanging Oneness within each individual. As god of death, Osiris is judge of newly deceased souls. He symbolically represents the spiritually whole individual, so his judgement is actually a type of self-judgement of the "ka" by the "ba"; of the "lower self" by the "higher self."

LIKE A RABBIT FROM THE DEPTH OF ITS HUTCH, BLINKING AT LIGHT, I HAVE COME. IN MY HEART A LYRE IS HUMMING. ITS STRINGS RING TRUE. MY BODY IS ROLLED PAPYRUS TIED WITH RED STRINGS THAT HOLD NO PRETENCE. I SHALL NOT SEE SUCH MISERY AND LOVE AGAIN. I SPREAD THE LENGTH OF MYSELF BEFORE FRIENDS AND GODS AND LET THEM STUDY ME. WHAT I HAVE DONE, NEEDED TO BE DONE. NO MALICE OBSCURES THE CRYSTAL POOL OF MY HEART. NO WORMS HIDE IN THE FOLDS OF MY SCROLL. I HAVE COME TO THE OTHER WORLD A PURE MAN. I AM WASHED AND FASTED.

The Arrival Egyptian Book of the Dead

ANCIENT GREEK HEAVENS

Kate Greenaway
1846–1901

THE ELYSIAN FIELDS, the heaven of the Ancient Greeks, were said to
be on the banks of the River Oceanus, or on the moon, or inside the
earth. Some saw paradise as the Isles of the Blessed, or the Fortunate Isles,
which Pindar pictures swept by ocean breezes, with cornfields and
meadows studded with roses and fragrant trees. The poet Hesiod (*c.* 700 B.C.)

says these isles are ruled by Cronos and there are three bountiful harvests each year. Horace declares that the corn grows by itself, honey drips from the oak, and there is no ungentlemanly trade and commerce.

In the afterlife there was believed to be neither day nor night, just a perpetual twilight. There is no time and so no ageing. The dead have no need of work, but amuse themselves with athletic games, riding, draughts, and playing the lyre. Life is easy. There are no storms, rain, or snow. The west wind blows gently all day.

Some Greeks imagined a meadow in the middle of a forest, where the dead loll in beds of flowers, while nightingales rain petals on them, scent falls from the sky like dew, and the trees magically supply glasses of wine. The dead enjoy a perpetual party: drinking from two springs, one of laughter, the other of pleasure; and indulging in free and open love-making, both heterosexual and homosexual. Tibellus says:

> There never flags the dance and song. The birds fly here and there, fluting sweet carols from their slender throats, while troops of young men meet in sport with gentle maidens, and love never lets his warfare cease.

AT FIRST ONE WANDERS AND WEARILY HURRIES TO AND FRO, AND JOURNEYS WITH SUSPICION THROUGH THE DARK AS ONE UNINITIATED: THEN COME ALL THE TERRORS BEFORE THE FINAL, SHUDDERING, TREMBLING, SWEATING, AMAZEMENT: THEN ONE IS STRUCK WITH A MARVELOUS LIGHT, ONE IS RECEIVED INTO PURE REGIONS AND MEADOWS, WITH VOICES AND DANCES, AND THE MAJESTY OF HOLY SOUNDS AND SHAPES. AMONG THESE, HE WHO HAS FULFILLED INITIATION WANDERS FREE AND RELEASED AND, BEARING HIS CROWN, JOINS IN THE DIVINE COMMUNION AND CONSORTS WITH PURE AND HOLY MEN.

Plutarch

ANCIENT HEAVENS

ASIAN HEAVENS

_L_IKE SO MANY cultures, the Chinese have pictured heaven in the stars, as an underworld, or in some distant earthly location. In ancient times, they buried dogs with the deceased to guide them safely to paradise, a task later assumed by mythical beings like dragons. Under the reign of the Chou kings (eleventh-to-third centuries B.C.), a cult emerged dedicated to T'ien, whose name means "Heaven," a celestial emperor whose court was made up of the souls of deceased nobles.

THE SKIN OF THE IMMORTALS IS LIKE ICE OR SNOW, AND THEY ARE GENTLE AND SHY LIKE YOUNG GIRLS. THEY DO NOT EAT THE FIVE GRAINS, BUT SUCK THE WIND AND DRINK THE DEW, CLIMB UP ON THE CLOUDS AMD MIST, RIDE FLYING DRAGONS AND WANDER BEYOND THE FOUR SEAS. BY CONCENTRATING THEIR SPIRIT THEY CAN PROTECT CREATURES FROM SICKNESS AND PLAGUE AND MAKE THE HARVESTS PLENTIFUL.

Chuang Tzu

Members of this cult believed that every aristocrat had two souls, that parted at death: first the "hun," an intelligent spiritual personality, which went to T'ien's heavenly court; second, the "po" or "vital breath," which followed the body into the grave and descended to Huang Ch'uan or Yellow Springs, a netherworld under the earth. Like the Greek Hades, this underworld was believed to be very close to the surface, and Prince Chuang is said to have paid it a visit by digging a tunnel. Commoners were said to have no "hun" and merely descended into the earth to assure the fertility of the fields. Despite many Chinese visions of heaven as a hierarchical court, the great Taoist sage Chung-Tzu says, "among the dead, there are no such things as lords, vassals, seasons, or tasks." He describes the "Chen-jen," the Perfected Ones, who were believed to be both physically and spiritually immortal. Preserved in "perfected spectral bodies," they could wander the earth and stars forever, and were often painted as birdmen, covered in feathers or sprouting wings, reminiscent of angels.

Some said that the immortals lived at the edges of the world, in a land of light on holy mountain paradises, like Mount Ku-she. Others claimed they inhabited P'eng-lai, an island somewhere in the East China Sea, where they kept the "Drug of Eternal Life"; a belief that prompted various emperors to launch fruitless expeditions in search of this fabled heavenly isle. Hsi Wang Mu, the Queen Mother of the West, was also believed to possess the elixir of immortality. She was an eternal being with the tail of a leopard and the teeth of a tiger, who lived on Mount K'un-lun, a mythical nine-layered mountain, believed to be the gates of paradise.

Immortals were said to ascend straight to heaven, without dying. Huang-ti, the Yellow Emperor, took his entire court and harem with him. The Prince of Huai-nan, a great patron of Taoist saints, ascended along with all his household, including livestock. T'ang Kung-fang, a petty official, received enough magic elixir to feed his family, animals, and daub his house, causing them all to rise up into the clouds. When people began to question why graves existed for some supposed immortals, it was said that these perfected beings died an apparent death and seemed to be buried, but actually no corpse was buried, only some personal item, like a sandal.

關來隱几枕書眠夢入
壺中別有天彷彿若
夷親面目大還真訣得
親傳晉昌唐寅為
東原先生寫圖

DREAMING OF
IMMORTALITY IN A
THATCHED COTTAGE
T'ang Yin Ming Dynasty

FOLLOW THE WAY OF HEAVEN,
    AND YOU WILL SUCCEED
    WITHOUT STRUGGLING.
YOU WILL KNOW THE ANSWER,
WITHOUT ASKING THE QUESTION.
    ALL YOU NEED WILL COME TO
    YOU, WITHOUT BEING DEMANDED
YOU WILL BE FULFILLED WITHOUT
    KNOWING DESIRE.
THE WAY OF HEAVEN IS LIKE A
    VAST NET,
ALTHOUGH ITS MESH IS WIDE, IT
    CATCHES EVERYTHING.

Lao Tzu

Tao Te Ching

HEAVENS OF
THE PRIMAL PEOPLES

*I*T IS WIDELY HELD among primal peoples, like the indigenous tribes of Africa, Australia, and America, that death is a spiritual initiation leading to rebirth in heaven. Black Elk, a Native American Sioux visionary, talks of "passing from this world of darkness to the other real world of light." In Ghana they believe the dead are "born on the other side of the veil." Among the Batabwa of Zaire, as a man dies, a woman symbolically gives birth to him in the otherworld, sitting back-to-back with him, on her heels with her legs wide apart, as if in labor.

The deceased are not just remembered by the living, but are also often guests in their homes, sometimes even having their own special huts. The dead and the living form a single community, with the dead simply regarded as having superior status. In the language of the Fon from Benin, the same word is used for "to be" and "to be called," and they believe that the dead in heaven who have no descendants to remember them will cease to exist. The Pangwe of Southern Cameroon say that while the dead live for a long time in heaven, they will all ultimately die a second and final death.

Many peoples believe that souls reincarnate in human bodies after a period in heaven, while other tribes populate an eternal hereafter with all of their forebears. The heaven of the Bazela from Zaire is a hierarchy of ancestors; foremost are the "inkolwe," the first-born, the founders of the tribe; then come the "basyekulu," the early sons, whose names have been forgotten in the course of generations; finally there are the "batata betu," the near ancestors. Each ancestor has the same status in heaven that he held while on earth.

Among the Tikopians, an Oceanic community, there are believed to be different heavens for bachelors, spinsters, married men, and married women. There is even a special heaven for lame spirits. All the inhabitants of the afterlife are able to visit each other, however, and the dead pass their time in eating, drinking, a little cultivating, and a lot of dancing.

THERE IS NO DEATH, ONLY A CHANGE OF WORLDS.

Chief Seattle

In Benin they believe that people go to different heavens depending on their role in society. When a king dies, he is said to have gone to Alada, the home of Benin royalty, to "be among his equals." In like manner, a dead soothsayer is said to to have gone to Ife, the religious center of soothsayers. The Algonquin of North America also say that there are various heavenly destinations for different social or religious groups. For the Tonga of Polynesia, it is only royalty and nobles who can expect to inhabit the idyllic heaven of Putotu; mere commoners can

HE HAS CROSSED THE MIRROR; FOR HIM NOTHING WILL EXIST IN THE DARKNESS.

Fon funeral chant from Benin

expect to remain on earth, turn into vermin, and eat the soil.

According to some African myths, heaven is a place where God seeks refuge after a tiring and difficult time associating with men. The Dagba of Central Africa say that their celestial heaven was originally linked to earth

WIDOW OF AN INDIAN CHIEF
Joseph Wright of Derby 1734—97

by a "very big rope," but God was forced to withdraw it because of the foolishness of the first people; this rope is now the Milky Way. Many other tribes also imagine heaven in the skies. The Maoris of New Zealand have a myth that after death a chieftain's left eye becomes a star, to watch over and protect his people.

The Aborigines of Arnhem Land in Australia picture the dead being rowed in a canoe to "Bralgu," the Island of the Dead, where they are greeted by other departed souls. Shortly before sunset each evening, the dead in heaven perform the important function of sending the morning star to Arnhem Land, by ceremoniously "kicking up the dust," which brings the night. During the day the star is kept in a "dilly bag" by its guardian, a spirit woman called Malumba. When it is released it flies up to rest on a tall pandanus palm tree, the Dreaming Tree of Life and Death. But Malumba has it attached to a piece of string so that it will not run away, and she pulls it back each morning, and returns it to her dilly bag. Most primal peoples see heavenly life as similiar to earthly existence. Africans talk of a village of the dead, much like those of the living, which may be stumbled upon by unwary travellers. The plains tribes of North America, like the Sioux and Pawnee, await the "Happy Hunting Grounds," filled with abundant game. The Admiralty Islanders of Manus near New Guinea believe that the dead retain their property and professions. The anthropologist Reo Fortune reports that, even today, if the dead man was a member of the native constabulary appointed by the Australian administration, he remains a policeman among the ghosts after death; there he receives periodic visits from a ghostly white officer of a ghostly white administration, and collects ghostly taxes from his fellow ghosts.

PUCKOWE, THE GRANDMOTHER SPIRIT,
COMES TO THE RESCUE

MODERN HEAVENS

JEWISH HEAVENS

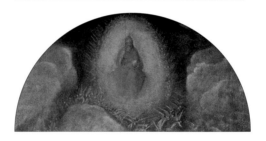

DETAIL FROM THE LAST JUDGEMENT: INTERIOR OF LEFT WING
Hieronymus Bosch c.1450–1516

NOTIONS OF THE AFTERLIFE in the Bible are very vague. The dead are described as going to She'ol, a kind of shadowy netherworld. The ancient rabbinical Jewish tradition tends to look to a future physical resurrection. Some held that the body would be resurrected from the "luz," an almond-shaped bone at the top of the spine, which would otherwise turn into a snake. Some Talmudic authorities suggest that upon death

souls are gathered in a "treasury beneath the throne of glory," awaiting physical resurrection. Under Hellenic influences, some Jews developed the idea of an immortal soul that could exist without a body. The first-century philosopher Philo Judaeus describes the souls of the righteous returning to their native home in heaven, and rare exulted individuals, like the patriarchs, going to the "intelligible world of ideas." The dead enjoyed a purely spiritual existence sustained in bliss by a fine luminous substance, which burnt the wicked. Other Neo-Platonist Jews speak of a heavenly "beatitude" in the world to come, as the climax of the soul's ascent toward God and its union with Wisdom. They believed that this was a gift of God, which could be attained by the devout before death.

> IN HEAVEN THERE IS NEITHER
> EATING, NOR DRINKING, NOR
> ANY BEGETTING OF
> CHILDREN...ALL THE
> RIGHTEOUS DO IS SIT WITH
> THEIR CROWNS ON THEIR HEADS
> AND ENJOY THE EFFULGENCE OF
> THE PRESENCE.
>
> *Rabbi Rav*

The midrash (or teaching) "Eleh Ezkerah," Legend of the Ten Martyrs, says that "all Israel has a portion in the world to come, except one who says there is no resurrection of the dead." It describes souls in a heavenly academy, eternally studying the Torah and listening to Rabbi Aquiva ben Yosef preaching on the matters of the day. Baal Shem, a proponent of Jewish mysticism known as "Kabbalah," said that God had taken Eden from the beginning of time and made it a heavenly paradise at the end of time. However, in 1885, the Pittsburgh Platform of the Jewish reform movement in America rejected as "ideas not rooted in Judaism, the beliefs both in Gehenna and Eden as abodes of eternal punishment and reward."

CHRISTIAN HEAVENS

$\mathcal{S}$T. IRANEUS, quoting a saying attributed to Jesus, says that "in the land of promise the wheat will grow with 10,000 ears per stalk, and the bunches of grapes will speak to the saint and beg to be eaten." St. Paul claims to have actually visited the "third heaven" and "heard things which may not be told or uttered." However, there is a tradition that he secretly described his vision in a book hidden in his home in Tarsus. The paradise he visited was said to include a river of milk and honey, and colossal palm trees with 10,000 branches, each with 10,000 clusters of dates and 10,000 fruits in each cluster. The Virgin Mary, Queen of Heaven, was said to walk among this splendor, with her escort of 200 angels.

St. Thomas Aquinas believed that in heaven, while we retain all of our other senses, we lose our sense of smell. Other theologians, however, were of the opinion that the dead are sustained on the fragrance of heaven alone, that must be sweet, according to an anonymous sixteenth-century poet who declares:

Within thy gates nothing doth come,
That is not passing clean;
No spider's webs, no dirt, no dust,
No filth may there be seen.

In his revelation, St. John the Divine was permitted to see "a door in heaven," and a voice that sounded like a trumpet told him to "come up here." He witnessed God, "like jasper and sardine stone," sitting on an emerald throne and surrounded by a rainbow. From God's throne flowed the waters of life, and on the banks of this river grew trees that gave forth a different type of fruit each month.

Around the throne were four strange animal-shaped spirits, each with six wings and many eyes. Day and night, these beasts sang, "holy, holy, holy, Lord God Almighty; which was, and is, and is to come." To the left and right were twenty-four lesser thrones,

IT IS NO FLAMING LUSTER MADE OF LIGHT,
NO SWEET CONSENT OR WELL-TIMED HARMONY,
AMBROSIA FOR TO FEAST THE APPETITE,
OR FLOWERY ODOR MIXED WITH SPICERY,
NO SOFT EMBRACE OR PLEASURE BODILY,
AND YET IT IS A KIND OF INWARD FEAST,
A HARMONY THAT SOUNDS WITHIN THE BREAST,
AN ODOR, LIGHT, EMBRACE, IN WHICH THE SOUL DOTH REST,
A HEAVENLY FEAST NO HUNGER CAN CONSUME,
A LIGHT UNSEEN THAT SHINES IN EVERY PLACE,
A SOUND NO TIME CAN STEAL,
A SWEET PERFUME NO WINDS CAN SCATTER,
AN ENTIRE EMBRACE THAT NO SATIETY CAN E'ER UNLACE.
INGRAINED INTO SO HIGH A FAVOR THERE,
THE SAINTS WITH THEIR BEAU-PEERS WORLDS OUTWEAR,
AND THINGS UNSEEN DO SEE, AND THINGS UNHEARD DO HEAR.

John Fletcher
The Celestial City

DETAIL FROM THE GARDEN OF EARTHLY DELIGHTS
Hieronymus Bosch c.1450–1516

NO MORE HARD TRIAL IN
DE KINGDOM;
NO MORE TRIBULATIONS,
NO MORE PARTING,
NO MORE QUARRELING,
BACK-BITING IN DE
KINGDOM,
NO MORE SUNSHINE FER
TO BU'N YOU;
NO MORE RAIN FER
TO WET YOU.
EVERY DAY WILL BE
SUNDAY IN HEAVEN.

Negro spiritual

occupied by elders wearing white garments and golden crowns; and behind them, hosts of angels "and the number of them was ten thousand times ten thousand, and thousands of thousands." There was no sun, no day and night, and no need of candles, for heaven was illuminated by the light of God.

St. Hildegarde experienced a mystical vision of God as a disc of brilliant light, encircled by nine choirs of angels. Dante echoes this image in his *Paradisio*, where he approaches God via nine concentric heavenly realms. All of these grand visions, however, seem cold and austere when compared to the more homely Christian heaven pictured in Negro spirituals:

EXCEPT YE BE
CONVERTED, AND
BECOME AS LITTLE
CHILDREN, YE SHALL
NOT ENTER THE
KINGDOM OF HEAVEN.

Jesus

> *When I get to Heaven, gwine be at ease,*
> *Me and my God gonna do as we please.*
> *Gonna chatter with the Father, argue with the Son,*
> *Tell 'um about the world I just come from.*

ISLAMIC HEAVENS

*T*HE ARCHANGEL GABRIEL is said to have guided the prophet Mohammed on a night journey through many paradises, culminating in the "seventh heaven." Here he was enveloped in a golden cloud and, in an ecstasy close to annihilation, Allah communicated to him the 99,000 ineffable words of the law and commandments.

AROUND THE PIOUS SHALL GO ETERNAL YOUTHS, WITH GOBLETS OF FLOWING WINE. NO HEADACHES SHALL THEY FEEL THEREFROM, NOR SHALL THEIR WITS BE DIMMED. THEY SHALL HAVE FRUITS SUCH AS THEY DEEM THE BEST, AND FLESH OF FOWL AS THEY DESIRE, AND BRIGHT AND LARGE-EYED MAIDS LIKE HIDDEN PEARLS, A REWARD FOR THAT WHICH THEY HAVE DONE.

The Koran

Muslims often portray heaven as the garden of Eden, a valley entered through an emerald gate. Heaven glitters with precious stones. Even the soil is "of the finest musk and saffron and ambergris; its little pebbles and rubble are gold." The blessed are invited to feast with Allah, and at the height of the banquet, Allah reveals himself in all his glory.

The dead are now all beautiful. They wear silken robes and "eat and drink with good digestion, for that which they have done, reclining on couches in rows." They are surrounded by splashing streams and fountains, which are never too hot or too cold. They drink from silver vessels, and are attended by graceful boys and dark-eyed, high-breasted "houris" – girls as lovely as coral and rubies. Luckily the deceased are said to have the sexual vigor of a hundred men.

THE ARCHANGEL MICHAEL

HINDU HEAVENS

*H*INDUS BELIEVE in reincarnation, and see heaven as only a transitory holiday on a long spiritual journey through many lives; a resting place where a soul reaps the rewards of its good deeds. In heaven there is no conflict and all desires are easily fulfilled, but this means that there is no opportunity for spiritual growth. A soul needs the friction of this earthly existence in order to move forward on the road toward eventual Enlightenment.

The *Brihad Aranyaka Upanishad*, an ancient scripture, says:

THE KNOWERS OF
THE THREE VEDAS,
THE SOMA-DRINKERS,
THE PURIFIED FROM
SIN, WORSHIP ME
WITH SACRIFICE, AND
PRAY TO ME, THE WAY
TO HEAVEN. THEY
ASCEND TO THE HOLY
WORLD OF THE
RULER OF THE
SHINING ONES.

Lord Krishna in the
Bhagavad Gita

> *As a worker in gold, taking an ornament, molds it to another form newer and fairer; so in truth the soul, leaving the body here, and putting off unwisdom, makes for itself in the heavenly state another form newer and fairer: a form like the forms of departed souls, or of seraphs, or of the gods...When he has received full measure of reward in paradise for the works he did, from that world he returns again to this, the world of works.*

Hindus believe there are many realms in the afterlife. Pritri Loka is a heaven inhabited by those who have performed sacrifices and charitable deeds. It is the home of the Pitris, the ancestors. Swami Sivananda says that souls in this realm:

...become gods and enjoy the happiness of heaven for a long period. They live with their forefathers. They come down through the spheres of air and clouds. They reach the world as raindrops. They attach themselves to some cereal or grain, which is eaten by some man who is fit to give them material to make a new body. Those whose deeds have been very good take birth in good families.

Svarga, the Bright Country, is a heaven of jeweled palaces, music, and paths of gold. Here the dead enjoy untold pleasures, attended by "asparas," nymphs skilled in the sexual arts. The heavenly "Place of No Hindrances," ruled by the god Vishnu and his consort Lakshmi, is described in the epic Hindu story, *the Mahabharata*:

> *It is made entirely of gold, and is 80,000 miles in circumference. All its buildings are made of jewels... The crystal waters of the Ganges fall from the higher heavens... Here are also five pools containing blue and red and white lotuses. On a seat glorious as the meridian sun, sitting on white lotuses, is Vishnu; and on his right hand Lakshmi, who shines like a continued blaze of lightning, and from whose body the fragrance of the lotus extends 8,000 miles.*

THEY EAT IN HEAVEN THE DIVINE FEAST OF THE SHINING ONES OR THE DEVAS. THEY MOVE IN CELESTIAL CARS. INDRA IS THE LORD OF HEAVEN OR SVARGA. VARIOUS KINDS OF DEVAS [GODS] DWELL HERE. CELESTIAL DAMSELS, LIKE URVASI AND RAMBHA, DANCE HERE. THE GANDHARVAS SING. THERE IS NO DISEASE HERE. THERE IS NO TROUBLE OF HUNGER OR THIRST. THE INHABITANTS ARE ENDOWED WITH A BRILLIANT SUBTLE BODY. THEY ARE ADORNED WITH SHINING GARMENTS. HEAVEN IS A THOUGHT-WORLD, A REALM OF INTENSE IDEATION. WHATEVER ONE WISHES, HE GETS AT ONCE, BY IMMEDIATE MATERIALIZATION.

Swami Sivananda
What Becomes of the Soul
After Death?

Hindus, however, see heaven as a sort of glorious, wish-fulfilling dream. The Theosophist Madame Blavatsky says:

> According to the growth of each,
> so is his life after death.
> It is the complement of his life here.
> All unsatisfied spiritual longings,
> all desires for higher life, all aspirations and
> dreams of noble things, come to flower in the
> spiritual life, and the soul has its day,
> for life on earth is its night.
> But if you have no aspirations, no higher longings,
> no beliefs in any life after death,
> then there is nothing for your spiritual life
> to be made up of, your soul is a blank...
> You reincarnate immediately, almost without
> an interval, and without regaining consciousness
> in the other world.

VISHNU AND HIS CONSORT LAKSHMI

BUDDHIST HEAVENS

*L*IKE HINDUS, Buddhists have many heavens, all of which are temporary rests between earthly incarnations. In Sukhavati, the Pure Lands, a heaven ruled by Amitabha Buddha, whose name means "Boundless Light," musical instruments grow like fruits on trees, that are brilliant with gems and gold; and "most excellent of all," a celestial coral tree rises up in "unrivalled majesty."

This paradise is a great plain, with rivers that are fifty miles wide, which create heavenly music which is "deep, commanding, distinct, clear, touching the heart, delightful, sweet, and one never tires of hearing it." The dead, however, may hear any sound they wish, including, for the wise, teachings of the Buddha that will help them toward the ultimate goal of enlightenment.

In one myth, Nanada, a Buddhist monk, is missing the wife that he has left behind to take up a religious life, and is considering returning to her. The Buddha is so concerned about Nanada that he takes him to the Paradise of Indra, the Bearer of the Thunderbolt. In this heavenly realm are trees that "display the splendid glory of all seasons all at once. Some bear manifold

THERE CELESTIAL NYMPHS WITH THEIR PLAYFULNESS CAPTIVATE THE WEARIED MINDS OF THOSE ASCETICS WHO HAD, IN THEIR LIFE ON EARTH, DECIDED TO PURCHASE PARADISE BY FIRST PAYING THE PRICE IN AUSTERITIES. THEY ARE ALWAYS IN THE PRIME OF THEIR YOUTH, AND LIBIDINOUS ENJOYMENT IS THEIR ONLY CONCERN. THEY CAN BE USED BY ANYONE WHO HAS DONE THE REQUIRED MERITORIOUS DEEDS; AND FOR CELESTIAL BEINGS, NO FAULT IS ATTACHED TO POSSESSING THEM. THEY ARE IN FACT THE CHOICEST OF REWARDS FOR AUSTERITIES.

The Heaven of King Indra

garlands and wreaths, fragrant, beautiful, and tied together, and also posies which fit the ear so perfectly that they seem superior to earrings." There are also such beautiful nymphs that Nanada forgets all about his wife, deciding to live the life of an ascetic and reap the rewards of heaven after death.

No one has mapped the worlds beyond death as meticulously as the Tibetan Buddhists in the *Bardo Thadol*, commonly known as *The Book of the Dead*. "Bardo" means "between-two" or "gap," and this scripture is a guide to the realms that are "gaps" between two human incarnations. It is studied by the living and read aloud to the departed soul after death, to help it through the spirit world. The *Tibetan Book of the Dead* tells us that the deceased see dull lights of various colors, indicating the realms in which they may be reborn:

AND IF THOSE BEINGS WISH TO INDULGE IN HEAVENLY DELIGHTS ON THOSE RIVER-BANKS, THEN, AFTER THEY HAVE STEPPED INTO THE WATER, THE WATER IN EACH CASE RISES AS HIGH AS THEY WISH IT TO — UP TO THE ANKLES, OR THE KNEES, OR THEIR SIDES, OR THEIR EARS....AND ALL THE WISHES THOSE BEINGS MAY THINK OF, THEY ALL WILL BE FULFILLED, AS LONG AS THEY ARE RIGHTFUL.

The Happy Lands

"devaloka," the realm of the gods; "asuraloka," the realm of the titans; "manakaloka," the realm of humans; "tiyaloka," the realm of subhumans; "pretaloka," the realm of hungry ghosts; and "naraloka," the realm of hell. A soul that is attracted to a particular light finds itself reborn in that world.

The Buddha, however, teaches that "enlightenment," not heaven, is the supreme spiritual goal. The soul that survives death is as ephemeral as the body that does not. Paradise is only a more pleasant form of prison; a transitory illusion that cannot last and leads only to another human rebirth.

BEYOND HEAVEN

ALL IN THE MIND

MATERIALISTS BELIEVE that a heavenly life after death is just a wish-fulfilling fantasy. Ironically, many mystical traditions would agree that paradise is a sort of dream state. "Gone to eternal sleep" is an inscription often found on tombstones – could it be that we die a little death each night when we fall asleep, and go wandering in the many worlds beyond this one? The Ancient Greeks represented this idea by making Thanos, their god of death, the brother of Hypnos, god of sleep.

Are there so many contradictory pictures of heaven because different traditions have glimpsed different parts of the other world, just as an alien visitor to earth may have gone only to Manhattan or the Sahara Desert; or are these visions culturally conditioned products of the imagination, like dreams, which must be interpreted

THE MIND IS ITS
OWN PLACE, AND
IN ITSELF,
CAN MAKE A
HEAVEN OF
HELL, A HELL
OF HEAVEN.

John Milton
Paradise Lost

symbolically? Many heavens, and the strange fantastic beings that populate them, certainly have a surreal dreamlike quality. The *Tibetan Book of the Dead* says:

> *Apart from one's own hallucinations, in reality there are no such things existing outside oneself as Lord of Death, or god, or demon, or the Bull-headed Spirit of Death. Act so as to recognize this.*

In the afterdeath experience, it describes souls encountering comforting "peaceful deities," which are symbolic manifestations of their good deeds; and terrifying "wrathful deities," representations of their fears and desires.

Much of what is pictured by ancient traditions can be understood only within that particular culture. Their images are alien to us, just as a Shakespearian character would seem strange to an Amazonian Indian. We no longer understand the power of animal totems, such as gods with the heads of birds and beasts, but this does not mean they are primitive or meaningless.

The Ancient Egyptian word "neter" is usually translated as "god," but it is easier to understand if it is rendered as "spiritual essence" or "divine principle." The many "neters" or "gods" of the Ancient Egyptians, like those of other polytheistic traditions, are symbols of the different natures of one Supreme Being. To use the mythologist Joseph Campbell's phrase, they are "the masks of God."

These deities also represent the spiritual potentials of every human individual, and many of the seemingly bizarre myths about heaven are metaphors for human spiritual development. An Ancient Egyptian text known as the "Cannibal Hymn," for example, describes the dead pharaoh chasing and catching the gods, cutting their throats, disemboweling them, and eating them – the great ones in the morning, the middling ones in the evening, the little ones at night. By doing this he absorbs their qualities, becoming the greatest of gods himself; a mythic representation of the soul's journey to wholeness.

If heaven is "all in the mind," is it real? The great mystical traditions of the world answer that it is real to those who experience it, just as this world is real to us; but ultimately both are dreams from which we must awaken. The Theosophist Howard Murphet says, "Death is part of the mortal dream of life. Dreaming that he lives, a man dreams he dies."

For mystical traditions, the supreme reality, sometimes called God, is like the light of a film projector on the screen of our conscious awareness. When we perceive that we are living in a film, we can turn and see the light of Truth that lies beyond both earth and heaven.

OUR REVELS NOW ARE
ENDED. THESE OUR
ACTORS,
AS I FORETOLD YOU, WERE
ALL SPIRITS AND
ARE MELTED INTO AIR,
INTO THIN AIR:
AND, LIKE THE BASELESS
FABRIC OF THIS VISION,
THE CLOUD CAPPED
TOWERS, THE GORGEOUS
PALACES,
THE SOLEMN TEMPLES, THE
GREAT GLOBE ITSELF,
YEA, ALL WHICH IT
INHERIT SHALL DISSOLVE
AND, LIKE THIS
INSUBSTANTIAL
PAGEANT FADED,
LEAVE NOT A RACK BEHIND.
WE ARE SUCH STUFF
AS DREAMS ARE MADE ON,
AND OUR LITTLE LIFE
IS ROUNDED WITH A SLEEP.

William Shakespeare
The Tempest

HEAVEN

THE DREAM OF ST. CECILIA
Paul Baudry 1828–86

SPIRITUAL QUEST

*T*HE LAST WORDS of the deaf composer Beethoven were reputedly "I shall hear in heaven." He pictured paradise as the removal of earthly sorrows and limitations. Shortly before his death, another composer, Vaughan Williams, wrote in a letter to a friend, "In the next world I shan't be doing music, with all the striving and disappointments. I shall be being it." Beethoven expected to hear the music, Vaughan Williams hoped to be the music, just as many people wish to be with God in heaven after death, but for some great sages and saints the ultimate spiritual goal is to be God.

The mystics discovered they were not separate from God, as the Creator and the creation; that all is One. As it says in the *Brihad Aranyaka Upanishad*:

> *This is to be understood by the heart: there is no separateness at all.*
> *He goes from death to death who beholds separateness.*

For mystical traditions, heaven is only another transitory illusion, because in the ever-changing world of duality, everything must transform into its opposite: pleasure gives way to pain, and pain to pleasure; life leads to death, and death to life. The Indian sage, Swami Sivananda, advises:

> *Abandon the idea of heaven. The idea of obtaining eternal happiness in heaven is a*
> *vain dream. It is a puerile idea.*

Beyond the constantly fluctuating world of duality lies the supreme unchanging Reality, which the Hindus call "Brahman"; all else is "maya," an illusion caused by the perception of this great Oneness as myriad separate things. Buddhists call liberation from this illusion "Nirvana." Although this state is sometimes given heavenly-sounding names like "harbor of refuge," "the cool cave," "the further shore," and "the holy city," these are only images and metaphors. "Nirvana" literally means "out-breath." It is the ultimate letting go, an enlightened state of Oneness with God.

The *Tibetan Book of the Dead* says that after leaving the physical body, the soul encounters the "Clear Light of the Void" that is Nirvana. All of life is an opportunity to awaken to this, our true identity, our essential "Buddha-Nature." The moment of death, however, is a particularly powerful spiritual opportunity to become enlightened. It is such a profound state of loss and change that the dead find themselves, for a moment, face to face with God. A soul that is spiritually mature, and has used its human life to develop wisdom and compassion, merges with the Love-Light and dissolves into God, like a drop of water into a mighty ocean. When asked if the person who attains Nirvana survives, the Buddha replied, "It would be wrong to say he does and it would be wrong to say he doesn't." The Hindu sages say that for an enlightened being there is no death, because there was in reality no birth. There is no one to die. There only ever was, and is, God.

IT SEEMS PROBABLE TO ME THAT IN THE HEREAFTER... THERE EXIST CERTAIN LIMITATIONS, BUT THAT THE SOULS OF THE DEAD ONLY GRADUALLY FIND OUT WHERE THE LIMITS OF THE LIBERATED STATE LIE.

Carl Jung
Memories, Dreams and Reflections

HEAVEN KNOWS?

*I*N THE PAST, heaven was often thought to be a place somewhere
beyond the known world, but we have explored all the earth and not
found it. Conventional science, the great religion of the modern world,
claims to have no need of God and is mute on the question of life after
death. As Emily Dickinson says:

> *Those — dying then,*
> *Knew where they went —*
> *They went to God's Right Hand —*
> *That Hand is amputated now*
> *And God cannot be found —*

But science can only explore the phenomenal world, not the human
spirit. Ultimately, life after death remains a mystery. In Corinthians, St. Paul
says, "What no eye has seen, nor ear heard, nor heart of man conceived,
has God prepared for those that love him," and Sir Thomas Browne
(1605–82) suggests that:

> *imagining a dialogue between two infants in the womb concerning the state of this*
> *world might handsomely illustrate our ignorance of the next.*

The great mystical traditions of the world advise us to cultivate an
acceptance of our ignorance, because this allows an openness to a deeper,
intuitive understanding of life and death, beyond our ideas and concepts. As

Stephen Levine says in *Who Dies*:

> *It is in the "don't know" mind that the truth is*
> *experienced in a spacious, timeless participation in*
> *being. Confusion is a pushing against a flow, a*
> *grasping at an answer, any answer. "Don't know" is*
> *just a space, it has room for everything, even confusion itself.*

To face death with more than just theories and expectations, the mystics say
we need transformation, not information; we must put aside beliefs about
God, and experience a direct knowledge of God. As the poet John Keats
puts it:

> *Wherein lies happiness? In that which beckons*
> *Our ready minds to fellowship divine,*
> *A fellowship with essence; till we shine,*
> *Full alchemized, and free of space. Behold*
> *The clear religion of heaven!*

At the end of the day, and everything must end, each of us must face the
mystery of death for ourselves. Perhaps this knowledge serves to remind us
of the mystery of our present lives here on earth. As Shakespeare has
Hamlet say:

> *There are more things in heaven and earth, Horatio,*
> *than are dreamt of in your philosophy.*

FURTHER READING

Aboriginal Mythology by Mudrooroo (Aquarian).

Adventures in Immortality by George Gallup (Souvenir Press).

Awakening Osiris – The Eygptian Book of the Dead, translated by
Normandi Ellis (Phanes Press).

Beyond Death by Stanislav and Christian Grof (Thames and Hudson).

Beyond Death by Howard Murphet (Quest Books).

The Bhagavad Gita – various editions.

A Book of Angels by Sophy Burnham (Rider).

Buddhist Scriptures (Penguin Books).

Death – the Final Stage of Growth by Elizabeth Kubler-Ross
(Simon & Schuster).

Heaven and Hell by Richard Cavendish.

Life after Death by Erica Simon (Sahni Publications).

Life after Life and *Reflections on Life after Life* by Dr Raymond Moody
(Bantam Books).

The Oxford Book of Death by D. J. Enright (Oxford University Press).

The Principles of Native American Spirituality by Timothy Freke (Thorsons).

Reincarnation – The Phoenix Fire Mystery, edited by Sylvia Cranston
(Theosophical University Press).

Tao Te Ching by Lao Tzu – a new rendering by Timothy Freke (Piatkus).

Tibetan Book of the Dead, translated by W. Y. Evans-Wentz
(Oxford University Press).